The Tame Ways of Wild Animals

IRMA RASPEL

The Tame Ways of Wild Animals

info@rockhopperbooks.co.za | www.rockhopperbooks.co.za

Copyright © 2024 Irma Raspel

All rights reserved. No part of this publication may be reproduced, stored in or introduced into a retrieval system, or transmitted, in any form, or by any means electronic, mechanical, photocopying, recording or otherwise, without the prior permission of the publisher. Any person who commits any unauthorised act in relation to this publication may be liable to criminal prosecution and civil claims for damages.

First Publication in 2024 | Rockhopper Books.

Print ISBN: 9780796159571
Digital ISBN: 9780796159588

Author: Irma Raspel
Illustrator: Annerina de Beer
Editor: Sunè Raspel
Cover Design and Typesetting: Caitlin Hewitt

DEDICATED TO EVERYONE CLOSE TO MY HEART, ESPECIALLY JOE, SUNÈ AND JOSEPH

WITH A BOOK IN YOUR HAND
YOU'LL ALWAYS HAVE A FRIEND BY YOUR SIDE

_____
My name

_____
This book is a gift from

_____
Date

CAMMIE THE GIRAFFE AND THE SWEET THORN TREE

It is a very warm day in the bushveld. Far in the background, you can hear the grey Loerie's song; even the birds are tired from the heat. Eddie the Eagle makes a sweeping turn in the air, his huge shadow visible on the ground. He is on the lookout for any small animals that are scurrying away from his strong claws. It sometimes seems that he enjoys this, because, of all the animals in the animal kingdom, he has the upper hand in the sky. A sly smile can always be seen on his beak.

On the highest cliff of the savannah lives the largest and oldest baboon troop. Billy Baboon, the leader of the troop who has been looking after them for years, sits and stares out over the plains. He is on lookout this afternoon, but he can feel in his belly that something is going to happen. He wonders if maybe it wasn't the many marulas he ate earlier. His wife, Amanda, warned him to not have too many, but how could he help himself when they are just so delicious? He peeks over his shoulder to the west and sees dark rain clouds rolling steadily closer. Sniffing the air, he licks his right pointer finger and holds it up high to feel the direction of the wind. He says to himself `Today is the day we have good rain again.`

The whole troop is enjoying an afternoon nap; the grownup baboons are snoring softly while the little ones try to keep quiet while wrestling each other. Every now and then, a mama-baboon will glare at the young ones out of the corner of her eye - that's their warning to quickly calm down. Billy decides to give his troop until the nearest shadow reaches the next rock before giving his first warning bark for everyone to find shelter from the coming rainstorm under the rocky overhang.

Billy can see far and wide from his spot on the high cliff, and this way he can see the interesting ways in which each animal prepares for the coming rain:
The meerkats flit back and forth building sandy walls around the entrances to their underground tunnels; the ants' commander is signalling like crazy to get the last of the soldier ants and the bits of food they collected into their nest. The spider seems to be literally rolling up her web, and the springboks sniff the air before gathering their little ones. In the distance, the giraffes are gracefully walking closer. Now, if he were not a baboon, Billy would surely have thought that they belong on the catwalks of Paris, with their long, graceful legs and fluttering lashes.

Billy knows that all the animals, from the smallest prey to the biggest predator, will soon come looking for shelter against the rain under the rocky overhang of the cliff. It is an unwritten rule of the bush that, when the big rain storms come, none of the animals hunt each other - this is the time when you need to keep your head about you, after all. Billy gets a fright when he realises how far the shadow has moved; he gives a loud bark and the whole troop moves as one to the cave where they live. Billy still has that uneasy feeling in his belly, but he brushes it off and moves into the cave with his family.

On the open savannah, Cammie the Giraffe and her family are walking determinedly directly toward the cliff with the rocky overhang. She heard Billy's loud bark and knows that her mom, Matilda, is now going to tell her to get a move on. They haven't been near the cliff for a while, and Cammie now remembers the nearby sweet thorn trees that were just starting to bloom and her mom's words that stuck in her head: "The sweet thorn tree has the yummiest, most juicy leaves you will ever eat." Cammie has never tasted leaves from a sweet thorn tree before and now couldn't wait to try them. She also remembers her mom's warning to take her time when eating leaves from a sweet thorn tree; those sharp thorns are not your friend...

Cammie looks behind her as she walks and sees a large dust cloud moving quickly in the same direction. She knows exactly who is causing it: Bob the Baboon and his troop of friends. Bob is the fastest and strongest baboon that Cammie knows, and, sometimes when she is out of sight of her mom, she lets Bob sit on top of her head so that he can see all the way to where the marula trees grow. Marulas are Bob's favourite food, but...oh no, it looks like our friends didn't notice how close the rain is! Matilda gives an angry snort in Cammie's direction and she knows that she now needs to focus and get to the overhanging quickly.

Every animal that is looking for shelter is almost at the cliff. Cammie is trotting next to her mom when Bob and his friend slip past them. Bob shouts to his friends: "We can't go the cave now! Uncle Billy and Uncle Bruce will have our furry hides if we only get there now. Let's rather go sit under the overhang, we'll be safe there." The baboon buddies take a few steps to the right and run like the wind.
Cammie sees the most beautiful sweet thorn tree, and it is as if it is calling her name..."Cammie...Cammie..." and with one long step she follows Bob and his buddies; not to go towards shelter but after the long-awaited sweet thorn tree.

Cammie comes to a stop in front of the tree, and right in front of her is the most perfect branch full of new leaves, the first in her young life that she is seeing up close. She hears and sees nothing else, just smells the delicious scent.

Suddenly there is a deafening clap of thunder, so loud that the rocks split and the earth shakes. This happens the moment that Cammie bites at the leaves from the nearest branch. Somehow, she manages to remember her mom's words: "A giraffe doesn't just bite the leaves from a sweet thorn tree, you wrap your tongue around the branch and carefully pull the leaves off." Cammie concentrates hard, tries her very best and finally savours the delicious leaves.

Suddenly, Bob and his buddies come running past, still frightened from the loud thunder that seems to hit so close to them. Still running, Bob shouts:
"HELLO CAMMIE!" and instead of pulling off the leaves, Cammie takes a big bite and immediately knows that this was the biggest mistake she has ever made in her young giraffe life: there is a thorn right through her lip! Cammie tries to focus, but all that she can see and feel is the long, white thorn in her lip. Bewildered, she tries to still her shaking legs. In the meantime, Bob gets the feeling that he should look over his shoulder and sees Cammie looking like she is trying to breakdance! It's just legs, knees and hooves, along with a pair of enormous, stunned eyes that don't know where to look. Bob stops in his tracks right there and his buddies, who just want to reach the overhang, crash into him and all you can see is dust, tails and chaos.
"Guys, look!, Cammie needs our help!" As one they turn around and head straight towards Cammie.

Bob's buddy Tobias is the smartest. He shouts 'Cammie, focus on my voice' and waves his arms like someone who is bringing in an airplane to land at the airport. Luckily Cammie listens immediately and focuses on Tobias' voice. 'Old buddy,' Tobias says to Bob, 'you are going to have to climb up to Cammie's head and be quick, this weather isn't our friend.' The dark clouds grumble above their heads.

With Tobias looking straight into Cammie's eyes and a friend holding onto each of her legs for support, Bob nimbly jumps up to Cammie's head and sees a big crocodile tear falling from each of her eyes. He whispers in her ear 'We have to work quickly; you are going to have to be brave and hold very still.' Bob remembers the secret that Billy taught him about taking out thorns: he stands on top of Cammie's long nose, digs his feet in, and with his tail crooked from the effort he calls his friend Sheldon to help. Sheldon also goes to sit on Cammie's head, digs his feet in behind her ears, grabs Bob's tail and shouts 'It's now or never!'

Bob grabs the thorn with both hands, Sheldon is pulling on Bob's tail and Tobias shouts from below 'Hurry Bob, pull out that nasty thorn!' Bob can feel Cammie shaking, but he digs his paws in deeper and pulls as hard as he can. He wiggles this way and that way, and won't you believe it, the thorn pop right out of Cammie's lip! At the same time, the wind picks up and the thunder rumbles and grumbles; every animal can smell the approaching rain. Before Bob can catch himself, he falls over but jumps up quickly and holds the long thorn triumphantly high as if it's a Word Cup. 'It's out!' he shouts excitedly.

All the helpers also jump up and hug Cammie, they are so proud of her.

Just then, Cammie's mom reaches them, her face full of fear. She realised that Cammie was no longer next to her, and now she finds her lying on the ground with a band of baboons jumping on top of her and dancing around her! Bob points the thorn like a sword to Tobias and says 'Take that, you silly old thorn!' Cammie's mom isn't angry, but she knows that they need to move quickly; the first raindrops are already falling. Bob says bye to Cammie and asks her if he can keep the thorn as a memento. Cammie is only too relieved. 'No problem!' she says.

At the top of the cliff, Billy and Bruce are standing in the wind, their fur blowing in every direction. They are very proud of the young baboons that they taught so well; they watched the whole affair from above. Bob and his buddies run past them into the cave and get an angry look from the older baboons, but this quickly turns into pats on the backs and congratulations for the young ones.

The rain quietly starts to fall over the bushveld. Every animal and bird, big or small, is safe and warm in their hollows or nests, or snuggling beneath a big tree. Cammie is cuddling next to her mom; her lip is a bit swollen and sore but she is very grateful for her friends who helped her so well.
She decides to always listen to what her mom teaches her and to think hard about her advice, and to always apply it better in the future.

LIZZY THE PYTHON GETS TIED IN A KNOT

The rain storm is over and all over the savannah there is joy, abundance and gratitude. Small rivulets become streams and find their way to the river that is milling and gurgling like chocolate milk being stirred.
The meerkats are out first. They timidly, but very curiously, look around. The rockjumper antelopes jump excitedly from rock to rock, bleating happily into the air. Deep in a dark hole, Mrs Patricia Python wakes up, yawns widely and smells the air with her tongue. 'Children, you have to be careful outside. This was a very big rainstorm. Stay on high ground and don't go near the big water snake,' she says. Funny that she would refer to the river as a water snake...

"'Yes, Mom!' Lizzy the Python shouts while slithering away lightning-fast to her friends. If you saw this odd group at a distance, you would wonder how on earth they became friends: Barry the bullfrog, Max the field mouse, and the Three Musketeers that consists of the termites Pete, Harry and Joe, make up the group. Now, to really understand how the buddies move around the savannah, you have to close your eyes and picture it: Lizzy slithers through the grass while Barry holds on to her neck with his short arms, Max holds on to Barry and the Three Musketeers hold onto Max's fur – and that's how the group of friends get around.

They usually meet up under the sweet thorn tree. Lizzy is there first, quickly followed by Max and the termites already on his back.
"Now we just need Barry," Lizzy sighs.
"Here I am!" they hear a voice coming from a pool of mud. They fall silent for a moment before everyone bursts into laughter and almost fall over on top of Barry.
"Come on, we don't have much time. We are riding the streams today and we have to hurry before they all disappear into the big water snake."
Like one man, or rather one snake, everyone jumps on Lizzy. Barry has to hold on tightly, but the mud makes it a bit difficult.

"We need to go higher up the hill so that we can really gain speed!" they all shout together. Lizzy's eyes turn into slits and she says
"Here we go!"
Halfway up the hill the friends shout "Go left!"
Lizzie turns and lands in the stream with a splash; the most beautiful stream they have seen in a long time.
"Hoorah, you go Lizzy!" the friends shout, and with a graceful turn they ride the stream downhill.

Everyone is holding on for dear life, their eyes and smiles both wide with laughter and joy. Lizzy makes another graceful turn and they ride the stream all the way down again, and again it was the most successful and fun ride ever.

The streams quickly dry up and the friends lie down on a warm, flat rock to dry off and bake in the sun. A distance away in the tall grass, they see Arnold Aardvark catching ants from an anthill with his long tongue.

Barry yawns long and lazily before saying "Lizzy, let's scare Arnold!" Besides riding the streams, scaring others and giving them a fright is their favourite pastime. The Three Musketeers shout as one:
"You're crazy if you think we're going with you. We might become lunch!"

Max makes a suggestion: "We'll all stay behind so that Lizzy can move quicker and more quietly." He gives Barry an angry look. He always starts giggling and gives them away every time they want to play a prank on someone.

Lizzy keeps her head down, her body close to the group, eyes narrowed. Determined, she slithers as quickly as she can through the grass. All that her friends can see from the rock is the slight movement of the grass, as if a soft breeze is blowing through it. Barry wants to start giggling and Max quickly puts his hand over his mouth. The Three Musketeers wave their pincers at him and say 'We'll pinch you in your side of you keep giggling!' Lizzy is almost there; her friends lean so far forward that they almost fall off the rock.

Lizzy is very close now; she can already see herself jumping up and shouting 'Gotcha!' The moment she wants to do just that, someone steps right on her tail! She gets such a big fright that she rolls away quickly, just like her mom taught her, twisting and turning in the air before looking back and seeing that it was Reggie the Rhino that accidentally stepped on her tail. When Lizzy hits the ground and wants to slither back to her friends – very embarrassed – she realises that she can't move! Her body has gotten tied into a big knot in her effort to get away.

Lizzy wants to start crying. What is she going to do now? She just lies on the ground with her eyes closed.

"Lizzy, are you okay?" Barry asks with a shaky voice. Lizzy peeks though her eyelids and sees all her friends who she loves so much standing around her; they also had a very big fright.

"What on earth are we going to do?" they all wonder in a panic. Mrs. Patricia Python can be very stern; if she finds out what happened to Lizzy, they would never be allowed to ride streams or play together again. Not far from where they are, lives the meerkat family. The dad of the family, Fred Meerkat, is very friendly and Max goes to ask him for help.

Fred Meerkat reaches the group of friends and quickly has to hide his mouth behind his hands to stifle a giggle, tears of laughter rolling down his face at the funny sight before him: Max and Barry are pulling at Lizzy from the front while the Three Musketeers are pushing her from behind. Fred is almost bent double from laughter at this comical team effort and quickly brings the whole affair to a stop. "Hold on, you lot!" he says, throwing his hands in the air. "You three, come here to the front."

Pete, Harry and Joe quickly run down Lizzy's long body and Fred notices how ticklish she is. That's why they always have to hold on to Max; their little legs tickle Lizzy so much that they don't get anywhere on their expeditions.

Fred has a plan: "You lot stand in front and sig to Lizzy."
The friends immediately link arms and start singing together "You got a friend in me...you got a friend in me..."
Fred cracks his knuckles; this is going to have to happen quickly and they only have one chance. The friends are already at the second verse when Fred starts tickling Lizzy up and down her long body. She laughs so much that her whole body goes limp and Fred can carefully undo the knot.

Tired from all the laughing and singing, the group of friends lie on the muddy bushveld ground and look up at the blue sky. Fred says fairwell to them as he's leaving "Enjoy the rest of your day, you lot, and remember: what happens at the flat rock, stays at the flat rock."

Arnold Aardvark has finished eating and is completely unaware of all the chaos that just happened right by him.

If you go walking in the bushveld, you might see a rare sight: a python with a frog and a field mouse holding on to her, with three tiny termites sitting on the mouse's head. This specific python has a flat tail now, but no one asks how that happened...

SOPHIA THE HIPPO GETS A HAT.

A Bushveld legend goes as follows...

Hippo really wanted to live in the dam, but King Lion said "No, you have to live in the river instead." "I can't live in the river, I will be washed away because my body is so round. I can only live in still water, and right now the river is very choppy," Hippo protested. "Where can I live?" he goes on to ask. Lion looks at Hippo angrily and says: "You can't live in the dam or the river, you are going to eat all the fish! What is then going to become of the crocodile and the eagle? What are they going to eat?" Hippo replies "I only eat grass, I promise." Lion shakes his head and says "How do I know you aren't lying to me?" Hippo shyly says "I will scatter my dung, then you can see that it contains no fish bones and that I only eat plants."
From that day onwards, Hippo was allowed to live in the dam.

Sophia wasn't your typical, everyday hippo. She was specially chosen to be the most beautiful and famous hippo in the world. She lived in the biggest pool in the river, because she needed the space to practice her dives and different swimming strokes. This really bothered the older hippos and the baby hippos, so Sophia was given a large pool all to herself.

One day, Sophia is floating on her back and looking up at the clouds. She is trying to make out what animals and shapes she can see in them. She is floating along leisurely when her best friend, and the biggest gossip in the bush, flies over and lands on her belly. It is Howard the Hornbill, with his pretty colours and long beak. Sophia peeks at him through her long lashes, her eyes blinking in the sunlight as Howard catches her up on the latest news. He is still telling her about this and that, when Sophia rolls in the water so quickly that Howard almost has to take flight to not get wet.
"What was that you said?" she asks. "A hat? What is a hat?"

Howard explains in detail about the hat he saw lying in the bush.
Sophia is immediately excited. "I want one!" she explains, waving feet in the air. "My cheeks are already getting freckly from all the sun."
Catfish pops his head above the water and says "Sophia, why are you kicking your legs so wildly? You almost flattened me!"

Sophia is so excited and her voice gets louder and louder as she explains. A few of the other animals come closer and listen carefully. Howard clears his throat and says "Let me draw a picture in the sand so that everyone can see."
Sophia rests her head on her paws and looks lovingly at Howard.
"Umf. Leave my tail feathers alone!" he says.

After a long explanation and planning all the materials they will need, everyone is ready to be given their tasks and get started. The finch family will be weaving and gathering all the reeds as they know where the best ones grow along the river.

'I want a Bushwillow seed on my hat,' says Sophia and asks Cammie to pick one for her.

'Oh, and Flame of Africa seeds, the red ones please. We can thread them on a string and put them around the rim of the hat.'

'I will get them; the tree grows right by our nest!' says Patrick the Porcupine. 'Sophia, you can also have three of my quills,' he goes on to say. Partick is actually very much in love with Sophia, but nobody knows.

'Thank you very much,' Sophia says. 'I really wanted some, but didn't want to ask.'

'The seeds of the African teak tree are so beautiful now,' they hear a deep voice say. It is Terry the Tortoise, the smartest animal in the Bushveld.

'And the camel thorn tree!' a little voice peeps from under a bush.

'Don't forget the carob seeds!' a deep voice says from the back.

'Well, there we go,' says Howard. 'Everyone knows what to get. We'll meet again in a week's time with all our materials. Finches, you get started on the weaving.'

The last thing that Sophia really wanted in her hat was an ostrich feather: a beautiful, long, white, ostrich feather.

'Who is going to ask Ozzy?' Howard asks the group. Everybody takes a step back; no one comes forward and volunteers to go grab the feather – you don't just ask Ozzy anything out of the blue, after all.

High up in the tree sits Bob and his buddies; they are just hanging around and listening to what the animals have to say when they notice the huddle...

Mrs Caity Blue Crane has the most important job: she has to measure Sophia's head. Betsy Finch flies closer with a long piece of grass and helps Caity to precisely measure Sophia's head.

It is two days before everyone has to arrive with all the materials. The finches are so proud of their hard work. They weaved a beautiful wide-rimmed sunhat pattern. That way, all the decorations that everyone gathered can carefully be glued on with the tree sap that has been collected in a rolled-up leaf and is already softening in the sun.

The big day is here! The sun is shining brightly, the sky is blue and all the animals are so excited. Everyone is there with everything they have gathered: seeds, quills, pods, everything! Everything, except one thing: the long, white ostrich feather. Everyone anxiously looks at Caity Blue Crane; she is arranging everything on the hat and the meerkat family is going to do the glueing.
Sophia is stamping her feet and batting her eyelashes from excitement.

On the other side of the veld, an urgent operation is being undertaken.
Ozzy Ostrich can feel in his bones that something is brewing. Every now and then, he can see a baboon popping up in the grass in front of him, and in the blind spot of his right eye he can see another baboon who is sitting and whistling Jan Pierrewiet.
What is going on? he thinks. Ozzy pecks at the rocks on the ground when he feels, oh no, there is someone sitting on his back! They are holding onto his dark feathers with one hand while pulling at his white feathers with the other hand. He spins around and sees that it is Bob that is holding on and grabbing at the same time!

His two buddies are shouting 'Only one feather, Bob!'
With one last pull Bob grabs the longest, whitest feather he can find, jumps down and lets loose towards the river.

Ozzy is so confused; he tries to regain his composure before anyone sees what happened.

The baboons arrive at the river just in time for the big moment. Sophia doesn't even notice that the white feather isn't in the hat.
"STOP!" Bob shouts and hands the feather over with a bow.
One of the meerkats put a dab of tree sap on the end and very carefully puts the feather in its place.

With loud applause, the hat is put on Sophia's head. There are even little holes for her ears to poke through. The animals rejoice, each one very impressed with how beautiful Sophia looks and proud of the part they played. Sophia's smile stretches almost right around her head and she spins around so that everyone can see the beautiful result of their hard work.

Sophia can't stop staring at her reflection on the pool. Nobody was jealous of her and only had compliments to give when they came down to the river to drink water. The impala ewes had the nicest things to say.

One lazy Sunday afternoon, Sophia falls asleep while floating in the shallow water and slowly drifts down into the deeper pool. She is sleeping so deeply that she doesn't wake up when her whole head goes underwater and her hat floats off her head...

When she does wake up with a big yawn, Sophie realises something is different and feels her cheeks: why are they so warm?

She realises with a shock "MY HAT IS GONE!" She starts crying so loudly that everyone who has planning to have an afternoon nap, or was already in the middle of one, startles awake and realises that they have a big problem.

Sophia is inconsolable; she is literally crying crocodile tears. Caity flaps her wings and Howard clears his throat before coming up with a plan of action. Eddie the Eagle receives the first task: he is to fly down river and look for the hat. Lawrence Lizard is also on his way; the rest stay behind with Sophia and try to console her and each other.

Eddie flies fast and low. His eyes are the sharpest around. Lawrence is swimming as quickly as he can without disturbing the water; he doesn't want the hat to sink and cause even more trouble.

Eddie sweeps around a bend in the river and spots the white feather. He gets closer and sees, oh no, the feather is dripping wet and done for! He knows how much Sophia loved her hat feather. He signals to Lawrence and shows him where the hat is. Lawrence carefully holds the hat in his mouth and swims back.

Everyone is still together waiting for news of the hat; even the little ones are trying to console Sophia. The Piet-my-vrou sings his famous song and the rock pigeon is cooing along to the melancholy tune. Suddenly the elephants trumpet loudly; they can see Lawrence getting closer with the hat and the wet, floppy feather. Everyone goes quiet. Sophia stops crying, but it just looks as if she is only catching her breath to cry even harder.

On the bank on the river, nobody has noticed that Ozzy is there too. He actually gets a little teary-eyed when he sees how sad Sophia is about the state of her hat. Luckily, the rest of the hat is still perfect. Ozzy stretches his long neck back and plucks the longest, whitest feather he has. He hands it over to Caity and says: "Let's make our hat perfect again." Everyone goes quiet; they know Ozzy can be difficult at times. Sophia stops crying. Caity puts the feather in the hat, and this one is even more beautiful than the previous one. The finches have a very smart idea: they cut a long piece of reed in two and bind a piece to each side of the hat. That way, Sophia can tie it under her chin and this whole affair won't happen again.

After all, afternoon naps on a Sunday are very important to everyone in the bush. Sophia looks just as beautiful as before. Everyone is overjoyed and spends the rest of the afternoon chatting under the big wild fig tree next to the river.

After this story, there was a strange new sight in the bushveld. Sometimes, just sometimes, you can see a grumpy ostrich pecking at rocks in the veld, and the strange part is that when he lifts up and flaps his wings to cool himself off, three baboons are sitting peacefully on his back, right among the soft feathers, and this ostrich has the longest, whitest feathers you ever did see.

THE WEDDING OF THE YEAR

A big occasion is one thing, but a huge occasion is a whole different thing altogether. Then you get an occasion of enormous proportions, and that is what is happening today.

On the plain grows the biggest baobab tree in history, anchored with deep roots that have survived many summers and branches that stretch so wide that a whole herd of elephants can stand in the shade. The baobab tree's name means "tree of life," and this is the centre of today's occasion.

Trees are very much alive, and one should never believe otherwise. Our baobab tree's name is Nandi, and she is the centre point of everything that happens in the animal kingdom: if something important happens, it happens here.

Nandi stretches her branches and lightly shakes so that her leaves that are covered in early morning dew can dry out in the soft, early sunlight. All the small animals and insects that have made her their home are also waking up, yawning and stretching. Eddie the Eagle circles Nandi and perches on one of her highest branches. He says in his deep voice "Nandi, this is a big day; all the animals are already arriving from far and wide. Is everything in order here with you?" Nandi rustles her branches and Eddie know that everything is okay. Just around the corner, the elephants are standing around peacefully, as they always are. But when you get closer, you can feel the atmosphere change into one of fun, excitement and festivity. Today, Franciska is marrying Hank; something everyone has been waiting for for so long. Franciska's mom, Irene, is dancing around excitedly; everything she has been planning for so long is coming together today.

On the other side of the plain, the elephant bulls are looking for Hank. They have looked everywhere and are getting anxious; they don't want the gossiping mice to find out that Hank is missing and tell the elephant cows. They will only get worried and trumpet loudly at them.
With this in mind, Ollie and Oscar, the older elephant bulls, walk towards the river, and there they see Hank up to his belly in a muddy pool, trunk and all! The two old friends give each other a look and call the other elephant bulls to help; this situation needs to be handled quickly. Hank gets a fright when he hears the call and looks up to see his dad and almost-father-in-law standing there, looking cross. In fact, Hank gets such a fright that he loses his footing and rolls in the mud. It's so slippery that he can't get back up. The older elephant bulls grab him with their strong trunks and Hank is quickly back on dry ground. They shake their heads and tell the younger bulls to fill their trunks with water. They all spray Hank down until he is clean again with not a speck of mud in sight. "Go sit is the sun to dry off, and don't move a millimetre!" the older bulls command. Hank and his friends go sit by the flat rocks where the sun is warmest.

On the other side, the elephant cows are merry and organized, fluttering and tiptoeing about. Irene has everything under control. The mice are busy scrubbing Franciska's toenails with loofas from the river. The birds are weaving reeds into a heart-shaped wreath to go around the groom's neck during the ceremony. The finches are the weaving experts and are supervising this very important job. The wreath has to be long enough that, when Cammie the Giraffe picks it up and stretches out her neck, it reaches the ground. The wreath is almost , and the birds are twittering excitedly.

In the meantime, in Nadi's shade, the ostriches are raking and sweeping the ground. The air is dusty and Nandi sneezes a few times; luckily the ostriches work quickly and are almost done. The beautiful flowers that Nandi grew with so much love are almost ready to open. They have to be fully open in time for the wedding and be at their most beautiful tonight. From a short distance, Ollie and Oscar walk closer with their trunks full of water. They nod to Nandi when they reach her; the elephants have a lot of respect for the mighty baobab tree. They spray the ground under Nandi where the ceremony is going to take place with water so that the dust can settle. Nandi lightly shakes her leaves and stretches out her branches; now everything is ready.

All the animals have arrived and are ready, from the mice to the meerkats and tortoises. Bright white rocks are lined up in two rows to make an aisle for Franciska to walk down to Hank. Everyone is very excited as the time for the wedding gets closer and closer. The apes and baboons have picked branches full of marulas and wild figs as refreshments.

Everything is going according to plan and Nandi is looking festive, ready for the wedding ceremony and reception. All that is now left to do is wait...

The gazelles are lined up next to the aisle, forming an honour guard. Caity Blue Crane is excitedly flying about while showing everyone where to sit. "Today, friend and foe sit next to each other; it doesn't matter whether you are predator or prey. We put everything aside for this special occasion."

Leonard the Lion is leading the ceremony and Reggie the Rhino will take care of the signing of the marriage certificate, which is made out of a slab of mud. Both Leonard and Reggie are esteemed animals in their region and are highly respected by everyone. Bob and his buddies are very excitable and are hopping around in Nandi's branches as if they are being paid to do so. Leonard takes his place at the end of the aisle, and suddenly there is a tail hanging down in front of him. This turns out to be Bob's, who is lounging about as if he is baking in the sun. Leonard swats the tail away with his claw, and instantly everything is calm again.

Here they come! The gazelles bleat loudly to announce the arrival of the elephants, and what a sight it is. Right in front, in her beautiful hat with a brand-new white feather, is Sophia, Franciska best friend. She is a bridesmaid and very proud of it.

With their trunks intertwined, Franciska and her dad come walking down the aisle. You could not find anyone prouder.. Ollie walks with his head held high. He knows what a pretty picture they make. All the animals are astounded at this momentous occasion that they have the privilege to witness. The finches fly down and carefully place the hart-shaped wreath around Hank's neck. Franciska has a string of flowers around her white ivory tusks, the petals dancing in the cool breeze blowing around them. Leonard clears his throat and the ceremony begins.

At the end of the ceremony, Reggie stands closer to the slab of mud that is to be the marriage certificate, and the newlyweds press the ends of their trunks into the mud. Max the Fieldmouse writes the date on for them with a small stick. The two trunk imprints look like hearts, and now Franciska and Hank have a special keepsake to remember the big day by.
The animals shout, whistle and bleat loudly; smiles all around. Leonard introduces the couple as husband and wife; they are now officially married!

Later that night, the animals witness the most beautiful sight: all Nandi's flowers are fully open, and everyone gathers around her in a big circle to watch a firefly land on each flower and light up the whole tree.

What an unforgettable sight!

However, one thing that was quite funny was all the different animals dancing with each other: An ostrich with a mouse, a snake with a frog and a lion with an impala.

That's the end of the story.